DATE DUE

The Revolutionary War

VOLUME 8

The Revolutionary War

VOLUME 8

The American Cause in Peril

James R. Arnold & Roberta Wiener

Grolier

An imprint of Scholastic Library Publishing
Danbury, Connecticut

First published 2001 by Grolier
An imprint of Scholastic Library Publishing
Old Sherman Turnpike
Danbury, Connecticut 06816

For information address the publisher:
Scholastic Library Publishing, Old Sherman Turnpike,
Danbury, Connecticut 06816

Reprinted in 2004

Library of Congress Cataloging-in-Publication Data

The Revolutionary War.
    p. cm.
  Contents: v. 1. The road to rebellion—v. 2. The shot heard around
the world—v. 3. Taking up arms—v. 4. The spirit of 1776—v. 5.
1777: A year of decision—v. 6. The road to Valley Forge—v. 7. War of
attrition—v. 8. The American cause in peril—v. 9. The turn of the tide
—v. 10. An independent nation.
    Includes bibliographical references and indexes.
    ISBN 0-7172-5553-0 (set)—ISBN 0-7172-5554-9 (v. 1)—
ISBN 0-7172-5555-7 (v. 2)—ISBN 0-7172-5556-5 (v. 3)—
ISBN 0-7172-5557-3 (v. 4)—ISBN 0-7172-5558-1 (v. 5)—
ISBN 0-7172-5559-X (v. 6)—ISBN 0-7172-5560-3 (v. 7)—
ISBN 0-7172-5561-1 (v. 8)—ISBN 0-7172-5562-X (v. 9)—
ISBN 0-7172-5563-8 (v. 10)
    1. United States—History—Revolution, 1775–1783—Juvenile
literature. [1. united States—History—Revolution. 1775–1783.]
I. Grolier Incorporated.

E208 .R.47 2002
973.3—dc21   2001018998

Printed and bound in Singapore

CONTENTS

CHAPTER ONE

Battles on the Frontier

The conflict between white settlers and Indians began when the first Europeans came to America. During the French and Indian War (1754–1763) the conflict was part of the larger struggle between Great Britain and France for control of the territory west of the Appalachian Mountains.

The Indians could tolerate the French. Large permanent French settlements were limited to the area in Canada from Montreal to Quebec. French trappers and traders traveled throughout the Indian lands to the west and south. The Indians welcomed them because they did not want the Indians' land.

The Indians could not tolerate the British. British settlers moved onto Indian lands and cut down or burned the forest to make way for farms and villages. With axe and plow the British settlers changed the land and drove off the game animals that the Indians needed to survive. As soon as the British settled one area, a new wave of settlers moved farther west. Some Indian tribes tried to live in peace with the settlers. Most realized that the only way they could keep their land was to fight.

Cruel fighting between British settlers and Indians had been taking place all along the frontier before the Revolutionary War began. British settlers had been moving along river valleys and through mountain passes into territory west of the Appalachian Mountains. The British government said that their movements were illegal because the land belonged to the Indians, but that did not stop them. The settlers showed no interest in living in peace with the Indians.

When the Revolutionary War began, settlers continued to move to the frontier. At that time the western frontier was in western Pennsylvania, present-day West Virginia, and Kentucky.

Kentucky: The Dark and Bloody Ground

A heavily forested region of the Ohio River Valley was known as the "Dark and Bloody Ground" before white settlers ever came. No Indians claimed the southern

The Indians and the British settlers had a long history of conflict and war. This painting shows the future patriot Israel Putnam being rescued from the Indians during the French and Indian War in 1758.

blaze: to mark a trail through the wilderness by making cuts in the bark of trees along the way

British settlers built cabins and cleared land on Indian territory. The quest for land caused most of the conflict between the settlers and the Indians.

portion of the Ohio River Valley, the area that later became Kentucky, but many tribes used it as a hunting ground. The region got the name "dark" because the thick forests had few clearings, and sunlight seldom reached the ground. It got the name "bloody" because various Indian tribes fought one another there.

In 1769 Daniel Boone began to explore Kentucky. Six years later, in 1775, Boone led about 30 men through Cumberland Gap to the site of what became Boonesborough. There, in the spring they built a fort. Boone went back to North Carolina to fetch his family and 20 more men. During his trip he **blazed** a trail (marked trees with a hatchet) that became the Wilderness Road. Thousands of settlers were to travel the Wilderness Road in what became America's first great migration west. In 1776 Kentucky became a county of Virginia, and Boone became a Kentucky militia captain. Also in 1776 the Cherokees and Shawnees started raiding (attacking) the white settlers.

Settlers on the **frontier** had to stay alert. In a painting called *Too Close to the Warpath* a young couple is surprised by Indians in the woods near their home.

frontier: the borderlands between European settlement and Native American lands in North America; the western edge of British settlement in the American colonies
garrison: the group of soldiers stationed at a fort or military post

The Indians later found a strong ally in the British. After defeating the French, the British had moved into the old French forts and trading posts along the western Great Lakes. The most important fort was Detroit. When the Revolution began, the British government ordered the commander at Detroit, Lieutenant Colonel Henry Hamilton, to supply the Indians with guns, ammunition, and supplies and send them south against the rebel settlers. The settlers believed that Hamilton paid the Indians money for the scalps they brought back. For that reason they called him "Hair Buyer" Hamilton.

Working with the Indians were white men or mixed-

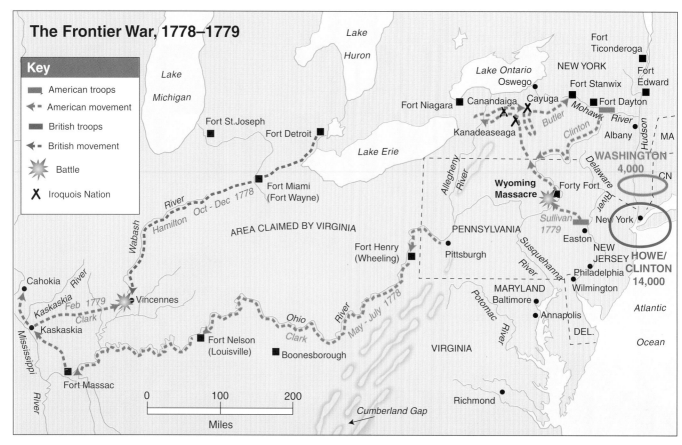

The Frontier War, 1778–1779

Key

- ▬ American troops
- ◀--- American movement
- ▬ British troops
- ◀--- British movement
- ✹ Battle
- ✕ Iroquois Nation

Lake Huron

Lake Michigan

Lake Ontario

Lake Erie

Fort St.Joseph

Fort Detroit

Fort Miami (Fort Wayne)

Hamilton Oct - Dec 1778

Wabash River

AREA CLAIMED BY VIRGINIA

Cahokia

Kaskaskia River

Feb 1779 Clark

Vincennes

Kaskaskia

Mississippi River

Fort Nelson (Louisville)

Boonesborough

Fort Massac

Ohio River

Clark May - July 1778

Fort Henry (Wheeling)

Pittsburgh

PENNSYLVANIA

Allegheny River

Wyoming Massacre

Forty Fort

Sullivan 1779

Susquehanna River

Easton

Fort Niagara

Canandaiga

Cayuga

Kanadeaseaga

Butler

Clinton

Oswego

Fort Stanwix

Mohawk River

Fort Dayton

Albany

NEW YORK

Fort Ticonderoga

Fort Edward

Hudson

MA

CN

WASHINGTON 4,000

New York

HOWE/ CLINTON 14,000

NEW JERSEY

Philadelphia

Wilmington

Delaware River

MARYLAND

Baltimore

Potomac River

Annapolis

DEL.

VIRGINIA

Richmond

Atlantic Ocean

Cumberland Gap

0   100   200

Miles

race white and Indian men. The settlers called these men "renegades" (people who abandon their own group for another; traitors): The Indians called them friends. The most famous and skilled renegade was Simon Girty. Girty and others like him helped plan Indian raids. The Indians attacked Kentucky again and again, sometimes with help from white renegades and sometimes without. The fighting between the rebel settlers and the Indians truly made Kentucky a "Dark and Bloody Ground."

George Rogers Clark

George Rogers Clark was born in Virginia and started a career of surveying the frontier at the age of 19. Clark was 23 years old when the Revolutionary War started. He was already an experienced woodsman and Indian fighter. He knew how badly the settlers in Kentucky were suffering, so in late 1777 he returned to Virginia to speak to such leaders as Thomas Jefferson and George Mason. Clark offered to lead an attack into what he called "Illinois Country," the land running from the middle of present-day Indiana west to the Mississippi River. Clark said that the Illinois Country provided the supplies for the Indian raids into Kentucky, and that he would capture the main supply bases. Jefferson and others persuaded Virginia governor Patrick Henry and the state of Virginia to raise money to support Clark's plan.

On June 26, 1778, Clark ordered his command, which numbered between 175 and 200 men, to board flatboats on the Ohio River. The expedition started at the Falls of the Ohio

A frontiersman rescues Indian prisoners. After the Revolutionary War popular paintings showed dramatic scenes like this while ignoring the way frontiersmen cruelly treated the Indians.

Left: A crowd cheers as Clark's flatboat, *The Willing*, departs Kaskaskia on the Mississippi River.

Below: Before joining Clark, patriots raid loyalists' property along the Mississippi River.

near present-day Louisville, Kentucky. They rowed day and night until they got within about 120 miles of the major British base at Kaskaskia on the Mississippi River, about 50 miles south of St. Louis. In order to surprise Kaskaskia, Clark marched his men over land through forests and swamps and across rivers. The march was so hard that the men had nothing to eat for the final two days.

The militia defending Kaskaskia were French. Clark knew that France was now allied with the United States. He persuaded the French not to fight and captured Kaskaskia without a battle. Another important base at Vincennes also fell without a fight. Clark was in a dangerous situation, deep in Indian country with only a

Below Right: Clark meets with the Indians and persuades them to stay out of the fight between the Americans and the British.

small force and very few supplies. Clark persuaded the Indians to stay out of the fight between the United States and Great Britain. He got supplies sent up the Mississippi River all the way from New Orleans. Then, he learned that "Hair Buyer" Hamilton was marching to attack him.

When Hamilton learned about Clark's invasion, he prepared to recapture the lost territory. He set out from Detroit on October 7, 1778. He led a very difficult 71-day trip through the wintry wilderness and recaptured Vincennes on December 17. The recapture of Vincennes satisfied Hamilton that he had done enough. With only 35 regular British soldiers and about 40 militia he rebuilt the fort and planned to rest his men there until the spring campaign season began.

At that time Clark's command numbered only about 100 men. But when Clark learned that Hamilton had gone into winter quarters, he boldly decided to attack. On February 3, 1779, Clark wrote to Governor Patrick Henry: "I am resolved to take advantage of [Hamilton's] present situation and [risk] the whole on a single battle. I shall set out in a few days.... Great things have been affected by a few men well [led]." Clark gathered 100 French militia and set out to attack Vincennes in the middle of winter.

The first 100 miles passed fairly easily. The soldiers lived off the game animals they shot. Then the march became tougher. The land was flooded, forcing the game animals to move to higher ground. The soldiers waded through deep icy water and had little to eat. Still, Clark's great energy drove them until they were within two miles of Vincennes. Clark led his tired soldiers to Hamilton's fort. He ordered the savage

Clark leads the way through the swamp in an area called "the drowned lands." The British-held Fort Sackville appears in the distance.

killing of five Indian prisoners in a place where the defenders could watch. This show convinced many of the militia who were defending Vincennes that it was better to surrender and live rather than fight and die. The next day, February 25, 1779, Vincennes and its 79-man garrison surrendered.

Clark had fought a brilliant campaign. He had conquered a vast amount of territory and done what he had set out to do. He even sent "Hair Buyer" Hamilton, with a heavy guard, back to Virginia.

Hamilton was put on trial for using Indians against the rebels, but Virginia justice proved true. Judges saw that even though the people of Kentucky hated him, Hamilton was doing his duty. They allowed him to return to New York City and rejoin his own people.

During the next years Clark tried to arrange an attack against the most important Indian and British base, Detroit. He was not able to do it. Although Clark and his men

Above Right: Clark's attack against Fort Sackville

Right: In spite of Clark's campaign, Indians continued to raid Kentucky and also laid siege to Boonesborough. In the defense of isolated frontier forts such as Boonesborough, everyone had to help. Women and children helped reload weapons and care for the wounded.

The negotiation to surrender Fort Sackville. "Hair Buyer" Hamilton wears the red coat.

Hamilton surrenders to George Rogers Clark on February 25, 1779.

had showed great courage and determination, the invasion of the "Illinois Country" did not help the settlers in Kentucky very much. For the rest of the Revolutionary War they struggled to survive against ferocious Indian attacks, many of them planned and led by white renegades like Simon Girty.

The Border War in New York

According to a treaty made in 1768, western New York and northwestern Pennsylvania belonged to the Iroquois Confederation. The confederation included six nations, or tribes: Mohawk, Tuscarora, Onondaga, Cayuga, Seneca, and Oneida. The lands of the Six Nations ran from Lake Ontario south to the Susquehanna River. The Catskill Mountains marked the eastern border, and Lake Erie marked the western border. Within this territory were villages and towns, many of which were large, well-built, permanent settlements. While the men of the

The Iroquois Confederation, the Oneidas, and the Revolution

Five Indian nations formed the Iroquois Confederation, known as the Five Nations, in northern New York around 1570: the Cayuga, Mohawk, Oneida, Onondaga, and Seneca. Around 1712 a sixth nation, the Tuscarora of North Carolina, joined them, and the Confederation then became known as the Six Nations. The nations had similar languages, of the Iroquoian group, and could understand one another. By forming a confederation, they were able to keep peace with one another, conquer other tribes, and develop an organized and prosperous society. Their system of government was carefully designed to prevent any one group from having too much power. Sachems, or "peace chiefs," from the different tribes voted and made decisions.

The members of the Six Nations lived in walled towns of more than a thousand people. European visitors called these towns "castles" because of the walls. The walls and the dwellings inside them were built of logs. The houses were called "longhouses." They had rooms along each side, with one family living in each room, and fireplaces down the center aisle. The Indians slept on wooden platforms. They grew corn, beans, and squash. They also ate fish, hunted deer for meat, and used the deer skins for clothing. The members of the Iroquois Confederation began trading with the Dutch in the early 1600s. They traded furs for such European items as kettles, knives, guns, scissors, axes, and cloth.

At the beginning of the Revolutionary War the Iroquois League had a total population of about 10,000. Before the first Europeans came to New York, the Oneidas had a population of about 3,000 living in four towns. Diseases such as smallpox, carried by European traders, wiped out hundreds of Native Americans. By the time of the Revolution the Oneida population had fallen to about 1,000. They tried to replace some of their lost numbers through the Iroquois tradition of adopting captured enemy Indians into their tribe.

Of the Six Nations the Oneidas and Tuscaroras sided with the Americans during the Revolution. The Oneidas may have chosen the American side because they admired Samuel Kirkland, a pro-American Christian missionary who had been living with them for many years. The Oneidas served as scouts and gave the Americans information on British troop movements. Some also fought alongside the Continental Army at Saratoga and at other battles in New York. Oneidas brought food to the hungry Continental soldiers camped for the winter at Valley Forge in Pennsylvania.

The Iroquois tribes fighting for the British took revenge on the Oneidas by capturing and executing several men who helped the Americans and by burning their most important village. The Oneidas who had lived in the burned village then became refugees. The Americans let the Oneida refugees live in army barracks in Schenectady, New York, for the rest of the war. The Continental Army had a difficult time getting Congress to purchase food, blankets, and clothing even for the regular soldiers: It was impossible to get Congress to vote funds to help the Oneida refugees. They suffered from cold and hunger until a former American general, Philip Schuyler, bought them food and blankets out of his own pocket.

After the Revolution the government of the new nation intended to protect the Oneidas' right to keep their land and to take land away from the Iroquois tribes that had taken the British side. But the governor of New York had other ideas about Indian lands within the state's borders. Between 1785 and 1845 the state of New York gradually took over all of the Oneidas' original homeland, forcing most of them to move to a reservation in Wisconsin.

Six Nations devoted their time to hunting and war, the women tended the fields and orchards. Over the years the Indian women had farmed the land with such skill that their fields and orchards provided ample food to supply the Six Nations.

Between 1756 and 1774 the British superintendent of the northern Indians was Sir William Johnson. The Indians of the Six Nations trusted Johnson because he treated them fairly and with respect. When William Johnson died in 1774, his son-in-law Guy Johnson became superintendent while some of his assistants, including Colonel John Butler, continued to hold important positions. When the Revolutionary War began, New York rebels worried that Johnson would raise the Six Nations against the Americans. The rebels disarmed Guy Johnson and his helpers and held some families hostage. Guy Johnson, Butler, and many other men from that part of New York remained loyal to King George. They fled to Canada for their own safety. Meanwhile, the Oneida and Tuscarora allied themselves to the American rebels, while the other four tribes remained loyal to the British.

Indians and Tories consider what to do to a family of prisoners that they had tied to a tree. Often male prisoners were tortured to death.

Lafayette went on a mission to upstate New York. While there he spoke with Indian leaders. Like many Frenchmen, Lafayette got along very well with the Indians. He persuaded the Oneida to send 60 men to join Washington's Army at Valley Forge. While Washington and Lafayette inspect the soldiers at Valley Forge, an Oneida stands beneath the tree on the right. The Oneidas served with Daniel Morgan's riflemen during the Monmouth Campaign.

The Johnsons, John Butler and his son Walter, and other loyalist leaders organized a base at Niagara on Lake Ontario. They gathered loyalists into military units and encouraged the Indians to help them fight against the Americans. John Butler described his goal to the British Governor of Canada: He wanted to "break up the back settlements" [the frontier settlements] of Pennsylvania and New York. Butler's plan led to a series of deadly raids in 1778.

On July 3 Butler, with a force of about 400 Tories and 500 Indians, struck the Wyoming Valley in Pennsylvania. The Wyoming Valley was a 25-mile portion of the Susquehanna River valley in the area of present-day Wilkes-Barre, Pennsylvania. Butler easily defeated the 360 militia and Continentals defending the valley. Butler reported that his men took 267 scalps. Then Butler lost control of the Indians, and they went on a rampage of killing, capturing, and torturing rebels. History remembered this event as the "Wyoming Massacre."

Above: Thayendanegea, known to white people as Joseph Brant

Left: This painting of the Wyoming Massacre shows the horrors of the border war in New York.

The Mohawk leader Thayendanegea, called Joseph Brant by the whites, attacked and burned Andrustown, New York, a settlement of seven families, on July 18. On September 13 Brant and 150 Indians, along with 300 Tories, attacked German Flats. While the settlers holed up in two forts and a church, the Indians and Tories burned 63 homes and 57 barns, and stole horses, cattle, and sheep. The patriots responded by destroying the Indian town of Unadilla, New York, in October. Their blow caused Brant and Walter Butler to lead an attack against the isolated frontier settlement of Cherry Valley, New York. The raiders were unable to capture a defended

Below: Indians destroy a rebel supply column.

fort and instead turned to killing defenseless people in their cabins.

And so the year 1778 passed on the border between New York, Pennsylvania, and the Six Nations. What made the year especially awful was the brutal behavior of both the Indians and the whites. The Tories in particular seemed to enjoy taking revenge against their former neighbors.

Washington Strikes Back

The frontier people sent appeals for help to Congress and to Washington's headquarters. Both Congress and

Washington wanted to help, but it was hard to find troops to spare from other duties. Finally, in the spring of 1779 American strategists developed a plan to deal with the Indians who were raiding Pennsylvania and New York.

Two small patriot armies were to assemble, the bigger one in Easton, Pennsylvania, and a smaller one west of Albany, New York, in the Mohawk Valley. The two columns were to join at Tioga, Pennsylvania, and then march into Indian country. Washington wrote the final order, which said that the American columns were to invade the homeland of the five enemy tribes of the Six Nations with the goal of "the total destruction...of their settlements and the capture of as many prisoners...as possible." It was a brutal order, but one that he and all rebels believed justified because of the terrible Indian attacks against the whites.

General John Sullivan commanded the column that assembled in Easton. His force included some fine Continental units led by experienced officers such as General William Maxwell, General Edward Hand,

Below Right: The experienced General John Sullivan commanded the American expedition in 1779 against the Indians.

Colonel Enoch Poor, and Colonel Henry Dearborn. There were artillery pieces crewed by the 4th U.S. Artillery Regiment, a small group of Morgan's riflemen, 120 boats for crossing rivers, and 1,200 horses to carry supplies. Sullivan's total force numbered about 2,500 men.

General James Clinton commanded the column that assembled in the Mohawk Valley. It numbered about 1,500 men and had over 200 boats. Clinton began his march to meet Sullivan at Tioga on June 17, 1779. He faced a major obstacle at Lake Otsego when the water level got so low that his boats were unable to move. The Americans worked out a clever solution by damming the neck of a lake, clearing the rocks and logs from the water, and then breaking the dam in order to float the boats on the flood.

Above: New York General James Clinton commanded the American column that assembled in the Mohawk Valley and marched to join Sullivan.

Right: An artist's version of Continental soldiers marching through a forest

Meanwhile, Sullivan's column made slow progress through some very rough terrain. A soldier wrote that the column marched through a wilderness where the trees were so tall that even at noon "it was as Dark as after Sun down." Some soldiers became discouraged at the slow and difficult progress. Officers ordered ferocious punishment to maintain discipline. One soldier had to run along a line of men from three entire regiments while the soldiers beat him with clubs and whips (called running the gauntlet). Another soldier was tied to a post and beaten 100 times with a whip. In spite of all problems, Sullivan and Clinton met at Tioga on the morning of August 19, 1779.

The Indians warned the British and the Tories that a large American force was about to invade their homeland. The British and Tories doubted that it was possible. They thought that the Indians were exaggerating. They sent two men to scout Sullivan's column. The rebels caught them, hanging one as a spy and the other because they believed that he had been involved in the killing at Cherry Valley.

American soldiers drive off an Indian attack.

When the combined American force invaded the Six Nations' territory, there was little that the Indians and Tories could do to stop it. One small fight occurred when the Indians and Tories tried to ambush the Americans. But the Americans were experienced fighting men who did not panic. They drove the Indians and Tories from the field, killing twelve of them while losing about 40 men killed and wounded.

Sullivan's Expedition, as it became known to history, moved from one town to the next. The Americans found the towns deserted and burned them to the ground: Chemung, "one of the Neatest of the Indian towns ... with good Log houses with Stone Chimneys and glass windows"; Queen Esther's Flats, where they destroyed acres of cucumbers, squashes, turnips, and corn with ears that grew two feet long and "watermelons and pumpkins such as cannot be equaled

Above: A Continental soldier sets fire to an Indian village while women and children flee.

Below: Settlers defending their frontier home

in Jersey"; and finally, Genesee, where they burned nearly 130 buildings. In all, Sullivan reported the destruction of 40 villages, including the crops and orchards.

Sullivan's Expedition did what it set out to do: It destroyed the homeland of the Six Nations. After the war a Seneca chief met George Washington and told him: "When your army entered the country of the Six Nations, we called you The Town Destroyer; and to this day, when that name is heard, our women look behind them and turn pale, and our children cling close to the necks of their mothers."

Sullivan's Expedition was a blow from which the Six Nations never recovered. The Indians had to live on British charity during the next winter. But Sullivan's Expedition did not put a stop to Indian raids. Instead, in 1780 and again in 1781 the Indians of the Six Nations struck back furiously to revenge their losses.

CHAPTER TWO

The British Look South

At the end of January 1779 the British were trying to complete the conquest of Georgia. British Major General Augustine Prevost had captured Savannah and then moved west along the Savannah River with a small 3,000-man army. He sent a talented officer, Lieutenant Colonel Archibald Campbell, to capture Augusta, Georgia. Campbell successfully took Augusta on January 29.

Small but savage fights continued along the western border after Sullivan's expedition.

The newly arrived American commander of the Southern Department, Major General Benjamin Lincoln, commanded an army of 1,121 Continentals and 2,518 militia. Lincoln marched his force from Charleston, South Carolina, to the South Carolina-Georgia border. His army faced Prevost, who was in position across the wide Savannah River. Lincoln tried to reconquer Georgia, but the British destroyed one of his invading columns at the Battle of Briar Creek, Georgia, on March 3. At a cost of only 5 killed and 11 wounded the British killed between 150 and 200 rebel soldiers and captured 170 more.

The British victory at Briar Creek secured Georgia for Prevost. He tried to move into South Carolina and capture Charleston, but Lincoln was able to block him. Then the summer heat came, and both armies ended active operations until cool weather returned. During the summer Lincoln made plans to cooperate with the French fleet led by Admiral Charles d'Estaing, who at the time was in the West Indies.

Operations in the West Indies

For Great Britain and France the West Indies were more important than the American colonies. Both nations had colonies in the West Indies that were sources of valuable resources such as sugar. Both nations enjoyed a rich trade with their colonies.

In 1778, after the allies failure to capture Newport, Rhode Island (see Volume 7), d'Estaing sailed for the West Indies. A British fleet beat him there and captured the island of St. Lucia. Then this fleet trapped d'Estaing at a French base on the island of Martinique. However, French reinforcements led by Admiral Françoise Compte de Grasse joined d'Estaing. They helped d'Estaing capture St. Vincent in June and Grenada in July. The British tried to take back Grenada. On July 6 the British and French fleets fought a large battle. Since the fleets had about the same number of ships of the line (the battleships of the Age of Sail), neither fleet could gain an advantage.

Above: Major General Benjamin Lincoln

Opposite Top Right: Admiral Françoise Compte de Grasse led French reinforcements to the West Indies.

Opposite Right: The French began their campaign in the West Indies by capturing the island of Dominica on September 8, 1778.

During the summer sickness seriously reduced British and French strength in the West Indies. Malaria and yellow fever, both carried by mosquitoes, struck hard in the summer months. Neither the British nor the French had enough men to defend all of the islands that they owned. Both sides learned that whichever side had naval superiority controlled the sea and could take and hold most of the islands in the West Indies. In 1779, before d'Estaing could use his bigger fleet to gain naval superiority, he instead sailed to Georgia to help the Americans attack Savannah.

The French arrived off the Georgia coast in September with 33 warships and 4,000 soldiers. They caught the British by surprise and easily captured several warships and supply ships. The British quickly went to work to build defenses for Savannah. However, Prevost had only about 3,200 men to defend the port.

D'Estaing began landing his French soldiers near Savannah on the night of September 11–12. Lincoln, with about 1,500 men, joined him on September 16. During the first attempt at cooperation between French and American forces, in the attack against Newport, Rhode Island in 1778, the American commander, General Sullivan, had been unable to get along with d'Estaing. Lincoln also found it very difficult to cooperate with the French admiral. Still, the allies slowly began to lay siege to Savannah.

D'Estaing agreed to spend no more than 15 days trying to capture Savannah. His men were suffering from sickness, with 35 men dying each day from scurvy (a disease caused by a lack of vitamin C). He worried that a British fleet might appear and catch him with many of his forces on land and too few still aboard his ships. Last, he knew that September was hurricane season, and he worried that a storm might strike. So, when the siege seemed to be going too slowly, d'Estaing decided to order an assault against the British defenses.

> **feint: fake;** a movement of troops meant to fool the enemy about what an army is doing

The French and Americans bravely attacked the British defenses at Savannah on October 9, 1779, but were driven back.

The attack took place just after dawn on October 9, 1779. American militia were supposed to make a **feint** attack to attract British attention, but failed. One of the two main assault columns became bogged down in the swamp and failed to attack at all. That left about 1,200 French and Continental soldiers to charge the British fortifications. One group of South Carolinians, led by Francis Marion, reached the top of the wall that protected the British defenders. Two officers placed a South Carolina flag on top of the wall and then fell with mortal wounds. A French aide to d'Estaing planted a French flag next to the South Carolina flag, and then he too fell. Another American officer replaced the flags and then was hit. Sergeant Jasper, the man who had replaced the South Carolina flag at Fort Moultrie back in 1776 (see Volume 3) while under fire from the British fleet, tried to put the flags up for a third time. Jasper also received a mortal wound.

The Polish nobleman Casimir Pulaski received a mortal wound while leading an American cavalry charge during the battle.

The attack failed with heavy losses. The allies suffered about 245 killed and 585 wounded, while the British lost only 40 killed and 63 wounded. About 650 of the allied losses were on the French side. On October 20 the French retreated to their ships, and Lincoln began the sad march back to Charleston.

The failure at Savannah was another allied disappointment and another blow against the ability of the Americans and French to cooperate. As had been the case at Newport the year before, the Americans and French quarreled about who was to blame.

The Spanish Alliance

When the Revolutionary War began, Spain controlled parts of Florida, the Gulf Coast, and the lands west of the Mississippi River. Spain also had many colonies in the West Indies and in Central and South America. Spain shared the French desire to see Great Britain lose power. After France became an ally of the American rebels, some Spanish leaders wanted to join the war right away. Other, more cautious leaders controlled Spanish strategy. They decided to provide money in secret to help the rebels but to avoid actual fighting.

When it became clear that Great Britain was not going to defeat the rebels easily, Spain moved closer to an alliance aimed against Great Britain. At the time Benjamin Franklin and the French Foreign Minister Charles Vergennes negotiated the French Alliance, they agreed to keep open a place for Spain if it wanted to join the alliance. On April 12, 1779; Spain allied itself with France. The two countries agreed to fight Great Britain until Spain captured Gibraltar, an important port on the southern tip of Spain. The British had captured Gibraltar in 1704; Spain had wanted it back ever since. Spain did not make an alliance with the United States. It never sent its forces to attack the British in North America. However, its powerful fleet joined the French fleet. Together the allied fleet posed a huge threat to England.

For the first time since the days of the famous Spanish Armada (fleet) of 1588 England faced the danger of invasion. The combined French and Spanish fleet outnumbered the British fleet. But the allied fleet suffered from inexperience, while the Royal Navy had a long tradition of victory. King George III urged his admirals to attack, saying "over caution is the greatest evil we can fall into."

Some British ships were equipped with a new invention that enabled them to sail faster and last longer. They had copper plates attached to their hulls. Wooden-hulled ships were perfect homes for certain kinds of marine life. Barnacles attached themselves to the hulls and greatly slowed the ships. Sea worms attached themselves to hulls and bored holes into the wood. Ships had to return to port often to have their hulls cleaned. The copper plates prevented barnacles from growing and worms from boring.

In spite of the British advantage, in August 1779 the allied French and Spanish fleets gained control of the English Channel. Their presence just off the English coast caused what became known as "The Plymouth Panic." For a number of reasons, including seasickness among the sailors and a shortage of supplies, the allies did not actually invade England. But the incident made

Spain did not fight alongside the French and Americans in North America. Instead, Spain seized British territory, including Pensacola, Florida, in May 1781.

a deep impression on British strategists. The British redoubled their efforts always to have a powerful fleet to defend the English Channel. But the Royal Navy could not be strong everywhere. By keeping a big fleet in the Channel, the British gave the French and Spanish opportunities in other parts of the world, including the West Indies and the American coast.

CHAPTER THREE

Campaigns in the North

*After Spain joined France in an alliance against Britain,
British leaders faced enormous problems. In the
Mediterranean Sea Spanish and French forces laid siege
to Gibraltar and threatened the British base on
Minorca.*

I n the West Indies the French had captured St. Vincent
and Grenada. The many threats all over the world
stretched Great Britain to the breaking point. The
British did not have enough strength to send important
reinforcements to the army and navy in North America.
The officer who commanded all British army forces in
North America, Henry Clinton, had to make do with the
forces he already had.

Clinton spent the spring and summer of 1779 with his
army in New York City. From time to time he sent small

Opposite Below: On July 4, 1779, the French captured Grenada in the West Indies.

Below: The large British army stayed inactive in New York City for most of 1779.

Anthony Wayne

Anthony Wayne was born in 1745 to a wealthy Pennsylvania family. After two years at school he worked as a surveyor, then followed his father into the leather-tanning business. Just before the Revolution Wayne was elected to the Pennsylvania legislature.

Wayne joined the Continental Army as a colonel in 1776. He quickly won promotion to brigadier general. During his army service somebody gave him the nickname "Mad Anthony Wayne." Different stories have been told about how and why he got the name. It has been said that "mad" referred to his being easily angered, always willing and ready to fight, or crazy. He was not at all crazy, but the nickname stuck to him.

Wayne led Continental troops in Canada, at Fort Ticonderoga, at Brandywine, Paoli, and Germantown, at Monmouth, Stony Point, Yorktown, and in Georgia. His attack on Stony Point is considered a prime example of his brilliant leadership. Wayne believed that fighting spirit, a willingness to fight, was enough to win a battle.

After Wayne helped drive the British out of Georgia at the end of the war, he stayed there to run a rice plantation on 800 acres given to him in gratitude by the state of Georgia. However, his plantation failed. In 1792 George Washington appointed Wayne commander of the small American army. Two years later Wayne won his most brilliant victory, against the Northwest Indian Confederation, at the Battle of Fallen Timbers. This victory drove the Indians from most of Ohio, Indiana, Illinois, and Michigan. Anthony Wayne died in 1796 while serving in the army.

groups of soldiers on raids against nearby rebel towns. Clinton also sent larger forces by sea to raid coastal towns. Late in the spring Clinton made one major effort to bring Washington's army to battle.

Stony Point, north of New York City, was important because whichever side held it was able to control King's Ferry, a ferry that crossed the Hudson River. The Americans used the ferry to move men and supplies from New England to New York and New Jersey. Stony Point was also the first rebel fortification that a British force would encounter if it moved up the Hudson from New York City in the direction of the Hudson Highlands. Stony Point served the rebels as an outpost (a small position that protects a more important position) for the defense of the Hudson Highlands.

On the last day of May the British attacked and captured Stony Point. But Clinton failed to bring Washington to battle. So, he returned to New York after leaving 600 men to hold the position. Water surrounded Stony Point on three sides. The British built a strong line of fortifications on the fourth side. The defenders were confident that they could easily hold Stony Point.

At first George Washington did not think there was anything he could do except "lament what we cannot remedy." Then Washington changed his mind and called General Anthony Wayne to a meeting. Wayne commanded a newly organized elite Continental unit made up of the light infantry from the entire army. Washington drew up a daring plan for Wayne's Light Infantry to storm Stony Point. They would attack at night and use the bayonet instead of the musket in order to surprise the defenders.

Just before midnight on June 15, 1779, an American force of about 1,100 men approached the fortifications protecting Stony Point. Seven hundred men waded through a waist-deep swamp to try to

Because they had to move through a marsh, the Americans made noise and alerted the defenders at Stony Point. A hard, brief battle took place.

surprise the defenders. But the sounds of them sloshing through the water alerted the British, who opened fire. A special force of twenty men reached dry ground and ran ahead to distract the defenders. Meanwhile, a force of axemen began cutting through the wooden barriers that were in front of the British trenches. Once the axemen opened a passage, the light infantry charged ahead.

A wild fight took place. Wayne received a head wound. According to a report published in the *New Hampshire Gazette:* "he was a good deal staggered, and fell upon one knee; but the moment he recovered himself he called to his aides...and said, 'Lead me forward. If I am mortally wounded, let me die in the fort.'" Wayne lived and remained in command during the battle. After 30 minutes the British surrendered. The British lost 63 killed, 70 wounded, and over 500 captured. The Americans lost only 15 killed and 80 wounded.

Washington judged that the Americans could not defend Stony Point again if the British made another attack. So he ordered the position abandoned. The fight

Below: The wounded Anthony Wayne (holding hat and supported by his aides) directs his light infantry over the British fortifications at Stony Point.

at Stony Point showed what could be done with careful planning and good leadership. Washington studied the other British positions around New York and decided that his men had a good chance to make another surprise attack against Paulus Hook, New Jersey.

Paulus Hook was across the Hudson River from New York City. Like Stony Point, water surrounded it on three sides. To attack Paulus Hook from the landward side, the rebels would have to cross about 500 yards of marsh and a water-filled ditch, and storm a line of fortifications defended by a 200-man garrison. Major Henry Lee, with between 300 and 400 men, led an attack against Paulus Hook at 4 A.M. on August 19.

Again as at Stony Point, the noise of the soldiers sloshing through a marsh alerted the defenders. But Lee used the same tactics that had worked at Stony Point, and the result was another overwhelming American victory. At the cost of only 2 killed and 3 wounded, Lee's men inflicted 50 casualties and captured 150 prisoners. Because it was so close to the main British army at New York, the rebels could not hope to keep Paulus Hook. So, Lee quickly abandoned it before the British could strike back.

The successful rebel raids against Stony Point and Paulus Hook were important because they gave the Americans hope and confidence during a year that was

Supported by his aides, Wayne looks at the field of victory at Stony Point.

The young Virginia Major Henry Lee led the attack against Paulus Hook. History best remembers him as the father of the famous Civil War general, Robert E. Lee.

full of so many disappointments. One of those disappointments took place far from Washington's army in Penobscot Bay, Maine.

Lee's men cross the ditch and climb the fortifications to capture Paulus Hook on August 19, 1779.

Defeat at Penobscot Bay

In the middle of June 1779 a 700-man British force built a fort on a peninsula in Penobscot Bay. The British goal was to use the fort as a base for raids against New England and as a safe place for loyalists to gather. They also wanted to collect timber for the naval base at Halifax, Nova Scotia. At that time Maine was part of Massachusetts. When the leaders of Massachusetts learned about the fort, they quickly made plans to drive the British from Massachusetts territory.

Massachusetts received permission from Congress to use Continental Navy warships that were in Boston. Commodore Dudley Saltonstall took command of the expedition that included 13 privateers and various ships belonging to the Massachusetts state navy and to private citizens. The ships carried between 1,000 and 2,000 militia and six small field guns. Lieutenant Colonel Paul Revere commanded the artillery.

Saltonstall's force arrived in Penobscot Bay on July 24. At first things went well for the Americans. The Continental Marines from Saltonstall's warships led the way. The Americans captured a British battery on an island near the main British fort and fought their way ashore near the British fort. If the Americans had made a determined attack, the fort would have fallen. But Saltonstall and the militia commander, Brigadier General Solomon Lovell, could not agree what to do next. For the next week the two leaders had frequent meetings that led to nothing. Finally, they agreed to set a trap for the fort's defenders.

On August 11 a small force of militia lured some of the British out of the fort. Fifty-five redcoats chased the militia into a trap where 250 militia lay hidden. The British saw the militia and fired a volley. The Americans broke and ran "in the greatest confusion imaginable— the officers damning their soldiers, and the soldiers their officers for cowardice."

After making his famous ride to alert the minutemen that the British regulars were marching out of Boston in 1775, Paul Revere served in the disastrous Penobscot campaign in the summer of 1779.

Continental Marines (wearing green uniforms) led the way during an attack against the British in Penobscot Bay.

The next day a British naval force appeared to relieve the fort. A few American ships tried to escape but were blocked by a British frigate. The rest fled in panic up the Penobscot River, where they were run aground and burned. During that campaign the Americans lost close to 500 men, while the British lost only 13. No American ship escaped the disaster. Later an American military court met to try Saltonstall, found him guilty, and dismissed him from the service. For the rest of the war the British kept a strong fort on Penobscot Bay.

Winter Quarters

After the American success at Paulus Hook there was little combat between Washington's army and the British in New York. Still, the autumn of 1779 brought Washington some familiar and troubling problems. The biggest problem came from the collapse of the Continental paper money. One dollar of paper money was supposed to be worth one dollar of coin (called hard currency). As time passed, the paper money became less valuable because people doubted that it could be exchanged for hard currency. In March 1779 ten Continental dollars were worth one dollar in coin. By the next spring it took sixty Continental dollars to equal one dollar in coin. Without good money the army could not buy everything it needed to get ready for winter.

For example, soldiers were still wearing the uniforms

that had been imported from France in the spring of 1778. After two campaign seasons the uniforms had been worn to rags. When Washington complained to the officials who were supposed to buy new uniforms, they replied that the paper money had sunk so low that their job was nearly impossible. When the officials received paper money that was supposed to buy fifteen uniforms, the money could buy only one. They also told Washington that the problem was quickly getting worse:

The Americans lost several fine Continental frigates and all the other ships that took part in the Penobscot expedition.

Continental soldiers build their winter quarters at Morristown, New Jersey.

44

Camp Followers

Both sides in the American Revolution allowed a number of women and children to travel with the armies. They were called "camp followers." They lived in barracks, houses, tents, or huts, usually separate from the troops. The women cooked, did laundry, and sewed for the troops, and also helped care for wounded soldiers. Some women were permitted to set up stands and sell tobacco, liquor, and soap to the Continentals.

When the armies moved, women and children were supposed to march with the baggage trains. The soldiers who drove the wagons were not supposed to let the women and children ride on the wagons, but most found it hard to refuse. Officers complained that the camp followers slowed the marches and took up wagon space needed for supplies. George Washington issued at least two dozen written orders in an effort to control camp followers. For example, in August 1777 he wrote, "Women are expressly forbid any longer, under any licence at all, to ride in the waggons, and the Officers are earnestly called upon to permit no more than are absolutely necessary, and such as are actually useful, to follow the army."

The armies recognized that it was necessary to allow women and children to stay with them. If they did not, soldiers might desert the army and try to return home to support their families. Many of the soldiers were so poor that their families would have starved if they were not permitted to follow the army. Some American soldiers lost their homes when the British army occupied their areas, so their families had no other choice but to follow the army. Both armies allowed a specific number of wives per regiment and gave them food rations. But the armies soon gathered more than their official allowance. Many soldiers picked up women along the way and married them.

Some of the women traveling with the armies were the wives of high-ranking officers. They chose to come along because they wanted to be with their husbands. They did not share the hardships of the wives of common soldiers. They had their own carriages and servants. Baroness von Riedesel, wife of a Hessian general, wrote: "I had still the satisfaction of daily seeing my husband. A great part of my baggage I had sent back, and had kept only a small summer wardrobe. . . . Our cook saw to our meals, but we were in want of water; and in order to quench thirst, I was obliged to drink wine, and give it, also, to the children." In her famous account of her travels with the British army in America the baroness wrote that there were only a few "ladies" present. She was referring only to the officers' wives, not counting the hundreds of "women," who were the wives of common soldiers.

About 23,000 British soldiers serving in America were accompanied by about 4,800 women and children in 1777. By 1781 that number had grown to about 7,700. An American officer wrote of the British army, "Their number of women and quantity of baggage is astonishing." A Hessian officer wrote, "The fact is that this corps has more women and children than men."

"we believe in a very short period, unless some extra-ordinary event takes place, the present currency will cease" to have any value at all.

The collapsing currency made everything difficult. The army could not buy food, shoes, or blankets for the winter. One American general wrote, "Many of our poor fellows have been two years in service and never had a blanket to this day." Most officers and men depended on their army pay to care for their families. When that money lost its value, many soldiers left the army to return to work so they could take care of their families. The terms of enlistment for 8,000 soldiers would end on May 1, 1780. Many who served out their terms had no intention of reenlisting. That meant that the army would shrink unless new recruits came.

Washington led his 11,000-man army into winter quarters at Morristown, New Jersey, on December 1, 1779. The winter came early, with heavy snow and cold weather. For ever after people called it the "hard winter." In fact, the winter of 1779–80 was the most bitter and longest of the entire eighteenth century on the East Coast. Half-naked, barefoot soldiers had to wade through deep snow to fell trees to make huts. Baron von Steuben had seen the hardship of Valley Forge. This was much worse. Steuben wrote that it was "the most shocking picture of misery I have ever seen."

There was so little to eat, and Washington reported that the soldiers ate "every kind of horse food but hay." The soldiers did not know how to cook such rough food. A Connecticut veteran, Joseph Plumb Martin, recalled: "all the breadstuff we got was Indian corn meal and Indian corn flour. Our Connecticut Yankees were as ignorant of making this meal or flour into bread as a wild Indian would be of making pound cake." At one point Martin went four days without eating. Men boiled their leather shoes and ate them. Some officers killed their pet dogs for food.

On January 2 and 3 a terrific snow storm struck New Jersey. Snow drifts piled up four to six feet deep, and the temperature fell. Nathanael Greene wrote about the soldiers: "Poor fellows! They exhibit a picture truly distressing—more than half naked and two thirds starved. A country overflowing with plenty is now suffering an Army, employed for the defense of everything that is dear and valuable, to perish for want of food."

A shivering Continental soldier wearing a ragged and patched uniform. A woman living in a nearby town wrote, ".... if the war is continued through the winter, the British troops will be scared of the sight of our men, for as they never fought with naked men, the novelty of it will terrify them, and make them retreat faster than they advanced to meet them."

CHAPTER FOUR

The Fall of Charleston

The British General Clinton had become discouraged and tired of the war. In August 1779 Clinton wrote to Lord George Germain, British Secretary of State for the American Colonies, that he had become "worn out by struggling" against all of the problems he faced. He wanted to give up his position as commander of the British army in North America and return home. Clinton suggested that Lord Charles Cornwallis replace him. While he waited for an answer, Clinton prepared a campaign against the southern states.

Ever since he had taken over as commander of the British army in America, Clinton had been acting on the defensive. He had led the evacuation of Philadelphia, the retreat across New Jersey, and the defense of New York City. The repulse of the French and Americans at Savannah had secured Georgia and opened the way for an attack against Charleston, South Carolina. Back in

Under a winter sky the British fleet gathers in New York Harbor.

The British fleet sailing from New York to Charleston.

1776 Clinton had commanded the army forces that had failed to capture Charleston. In the fall of 1779 he decided to take personal command of the second expedition against Charleston. Cornwallis would act as his second in command.

In order to avoid having his forces spread too thin, Clinton ordered the evacuation of Newport, Rhode Island. The garrison moved to New York to reinforce the main army. Then Clinton left the able German general, Wilhelm von Knyphausen, in charge of the defense of New York. The day after Christmas, December 26, 1779, a huge convoy of 90 transports sailed from New York Harbor for Charleston. The transports carried an army of 8,500 men plus supplies, equipment, and animals. Terrible winter storms battered the convoy for more than a month. Masts snapped, sails shredded, ships began to leak. The poor horses stored below decks suffered. Many broke their legs when the ships rolled about in the high waves. They had to be destroyed.

Abraham Whipple was considered to be Rhode Island's most experienced sea captain. In July 1779 Whipple had the good fortune to capture and bring to Boston eight valuable British merchant ships. The sale of the ships made Whipple rich.

A transport carrying all of Clinton's artillery sank. Two frigates also went down. One transport lost all of its masts. It drifted helplessly for eleven weeks until it blew ashore in Cornwall, England, 3,000 miles on the other side of the Atlantic Ocean. The rest of the battered fleet finally reached the South Carolina coast at the end of January 1780. On February 11, 1780, Clinton's army began landing 30 miles south of Charleston.

Charleston lay on a peninsula between the Ashley and Cooper rivers. In order to defend Charleston, the patriot forces had to do two things. They had to prevent enemy ships from crossing the bar and entering the harbor. Two forts, Fort Moultrie and Fort Johnson, defended the bar. Back in 1776 Fort Moultrie had successfully kept the British fleet from entering the harbor. The defenders also had to keep control of Charleston Neck, a mile-and-a-half-wide land bridge between the Ashley and Cooper rivers that connected the city with the rest of the state.

Like a Roman emperor in ancient times, the South Carolina assembly gave Governor John Rutledge emergency dictatorial powers. Rutledge called out the militia and began seizing property needed to defend the city. Included in that property were 600 slaves whom Rutledge ordered to build a defensive line across Charleston neck to protect the city from an attack by land. General Benjamin

Lincoln took command of the soldiers who defended that line.

Lincoln was uncertain if he should try to defend Charleston. He knew that Clinton's forces outnumbered his own. Lincoln wanted to abandon Charleston in order to save his 5,500-man army. But Charleston's political leaders pointed out that the

British siege lines outside of Charleston. In the distance the British fleet bombards the city.

defenses had worked just fine back in 1776 and that they should work again. Lincoln unwisely decided to stay in Charleston.

Congress had sent Commodore Abraham Whipple to command a small fleet of Continental navy ships to help defend Charleston. Whipple doubted that the forts could again keep the British navy away from the harbor. Whipple also knew that he was too weak to fight the British fleet. So Whipple withdrew his ships into the Cooper River. He sank some of them in order to help make a log-and-chain barrier and anchored his other ships so they could fire over the barrier. In that way Whipple prevented British warships from sailing up the Cooper River and firing into the rear of the American defenses.

On March 6 Clinton sent a force to attack Fort Johnson from the landward side. The defenders abandoned the fort and thus opened the harbor to British ships. Next Clinton ordered his army to march across the Ashley River onto Charleston Neck. Lincoln expected the British to cross at Ashley Ferry, and there the rebels built defenses. Instead, Clinton secretly moved boats into position three miles above the ferry in order to cross the river. His clever move outflanked the defenders of Ashley Ferry and forced them to retreat to Charleston. So, Clinton had outwitted Lincoln and overcome the best American defensive position at the Ashley River. Then Clinton moved toward the city and began building siege lines (trenches and small dirt forts) facing the city's landward defenses. On April 8 British warships ran past Fort Moultrie and anchored in the harbor. The defenders in Charleston were surrounded and almost trapped.

Clinton's moves had surprised Benjamin Lincoln. He had not expected the British to maneuver in that way. Because of Whipple's barrier on the Cooper River Lincoln still could escape from the city by moving his men across the river. An American force of 500 men defended this escape hatch at a small crossroads called Monck's Corner.

Clinton wanted to close the trap. He sent a force that included Lieutenant Colonel Banastre Tarleton with a unit of Tory cavalry, the British Legion, to attack the

Opposite Top: Lieutenant Colonel Banastre Tarleton became the most feared British cavalry leader in the south.

quarter: mercy to a surrendered enemy; to give quarter is to spare the life of an enemy who has surrendered or to allow an enemy to surrender

Opposite Below: The surrender at Charleston destroyed the largest force of Continental soldiers in the south.

rebels at Monck's Corner. Tarleton performed his mission very well. Tarleton attacked at 3 A.M. on April 14 and caught the rebels by surprise. Tarleton scattered the rebel force, killing and wounding 20, capturing 67, and most importantly, also capturing 42 loaded wagons and almost 300 horses.

At this fight Tarleton's men began to earn a reputation for brutality. They seemed unwilling to stop fighting after an enemy force surrendered. A British officer wrote that an American major "was mangled in the most shocking manner. He had several wounds, a severe one behind his ear. This unfortunate officer lived several hours...and even in his last moments cursing the British for their barbarity in having refused **quarter** [meaning refused to stop fighting] after he had surrendered." In fact, Tarleton's men had taken 67 prisoners. Still, the word spread among patriots that Tarleton's men were savage fighters.

After the difficult voyage from New York the British lacked wagons and horses. Tarleton's little victory helped solve this problem. More importantly, after the fight at Monck's Corner British forces marched down the Cooper River and closed the trap around the rebel defenders of Charleston.

By April 19 Clinton's siege lines across the Charleston Neck had moved to within 200 yards of the American position. On May 6 British marines forced the surrender of Fort Moultrie. A few days later Charleston endured a ferocious bombardment that broke the spirit of the town leaders. They urged Lincoln to surrender to save their city from destruction. On May 12, 1780, some 5,500 American Continentals and militia surrendered. It was the largest surrender of American forces during the Revolutionary War and the third largest in all of American history (the two largest would take place during World War Two).

For Clinton the capture of Charleston was a triumph. It was the greatest British victory against the rebels until that time. Clinton deserved the credit because he had displayed excellent strategy and cooperated very well with the Royal Navy. At very little cost he had captured a valuable base for a campaign to reconquer the south. Clinton left Major General Charles Cornwallis in command of British operations in the south. Clinton then returned to New York City in June.

The loss of Charleston was a disaster for the rebel cause in the south. Tarleton kept the pressure on the rebels. Colonel Abraham Buford commanded the last force of Continentals in South Carolina. To catch them, Tarleton chose a cavalry force, had foot soldiers ride double on the back of the cavalry horses, and set out on a very fast march against Buford. Tarleton's force covered 105 miles in 54 hours. Even though Buford outnumbered him two to one, Tarleton attacked on May 29 at a place called Waxhaws and nearly destroyed Buford's Continentals.

British troops commanded by Tarleton slaughtering Continentals at Waxhaws.

The Americans again claimed that Tarleton's men refused to accept the surrender of the Americans and instead killed them in cold blood. What is certain is that the fight at Waxhaws made Tarleton a British hero and a hated American enemy. The *London Chronicle* accepted that war was brutal and did not blame Tarleton. It wrote, "Colonel Tarleton knew, that having taken a command of the King's troops, the duty he owed to his country directed him to fight and conquer." The patriots looked at it differently and called the slaughter of surrendered men "Tarleton's Quarter" (in the Revolutionary War, to give someone the chance to surrender was to give them "quarter") and called the man himself "Bloody Tarleton."

CHAPTER FIVE

Disaster at Camden

Early in 1780 French officials warned Congress that the United States should not sit and wait for the French to win the war for them. Congress responded by sending General Johann Kalb (often called Baron de Kalb although he was not a baron) with a small Continental force south to the Carolinas. Congress hoped that Kalb's Continentals would provide a rallying point for the southern militia.

Johann Kalb led a remarkable march of Maryland and Delaware Continentals from Morristown, New Jersey, to South Carolina. Even though they often marched 15 to 18 miles a day, they arrived too late to save Charleston.

Kalb's men were already marching south when Congress learned of the loss of Charleston. Congress chose Major General Horatio Gates to take command of the Southern Department. Congress hoped that Gates could do what he had done at Saratoga: rally the militia and beat the British. Congress did not ask George Washington for any advice when it chose Gates. If Congress had asked, Washington would have recommended General Nathanael Greene. Gates himself had doubts about his new assignment. He complained that his job was to take "the command of an army without strength, a military chest without money, a Department apparently deficient in public spirit," and all of this in a climate that he believed was so bad that it increased depression instead of encouraging fighting spirit.

Meanwhile, in the south Tarleton's victory at Waxhaws had wiped out the last organized patriot military force in Georgia and the Carolinas. General Cornwallis, with about 8,000 men, was left with the job of securing the region. He left strong garrisons in Savannah and

The talented and aggressive Major General Lord Charles Cornwallis took charge of British forces in the south after Clinton returned to New York.

Charleston and moved inland to conquer the rest of the Carolinas. Some of his soldiers moved west as far as Ninety-Six, a small town that controlled western South Carolina, while Cornwallis sent a bigger group to Camden, South Carolina.

Cornwallis had to control a large area with too few men. American partisans (during the Revolutionary War guerrillas were called "partisans") had organized in the Georgia and Carolina back country (the wild land between the mountains and the coastal plain). To the British it seemed as if partisan attacks could strike at any time and any place. For that reason Cornwallis had to scatter forces among twelve towns and forts in order to protect his supply line leading back to Charleston. Sickness also weakened Cornwallis's forces. By the time a force commanded by Lord Rawdon reached Camden to set up a base, 800 men were sick. The British built a hospital at Camden to shelter the sick.

Gates arrived at Coxe's Mill, North Carolina, on July 25, 1780. There he found Kalb with a force of about 1,200 Continentals. The Americans were in poor shape. They had little food and few supplies, and many were sick. Still, Gates ordered the army to march against Camden. He ignored advice and chose a route that went through barren country where his men could not find food. His men lived on green peaches and green corn. They were so weak that it took them two weeks to cover 120 miles.

By the time Gates got close to Camden, he had been joined by militia and by a handful of Continentals who had survived earlier battles. Gates thought that his army numbered between 6,000 and 7,000 men. One of Gates's officers made a list of the soldiers fit for duty and reported that he had only 3,052 men. Gates looked at the list and said, "There are enough for our purpose." Gates ordered a night march against Camden to begin on August 15.

The rebels had gathered some food before the march. Because there was a plentiful supply of molasses, Gates ordered that all the soldiers receive a one-quarter pint drink. The soldiers ate and drank and began the march. The molasses caused diarrhea in hundreds of soldiers. An officer wrote that men were "breaking the ranks all night [to relieve themselves] and were certainly much [weakened] before the action commenced in the morning."

The armies collided about 2:30 A.M. on August 16, 1780. Both armies deployed (moved off the road) into battle formation. Because of swamps on both sides of the road the battlefield was only about one mile wide. Gates placed all of his Continentals on his right and his militia on his left. That was a fatal mistake.

General Horatio Gates made too many mistakes during the Camden campaign.

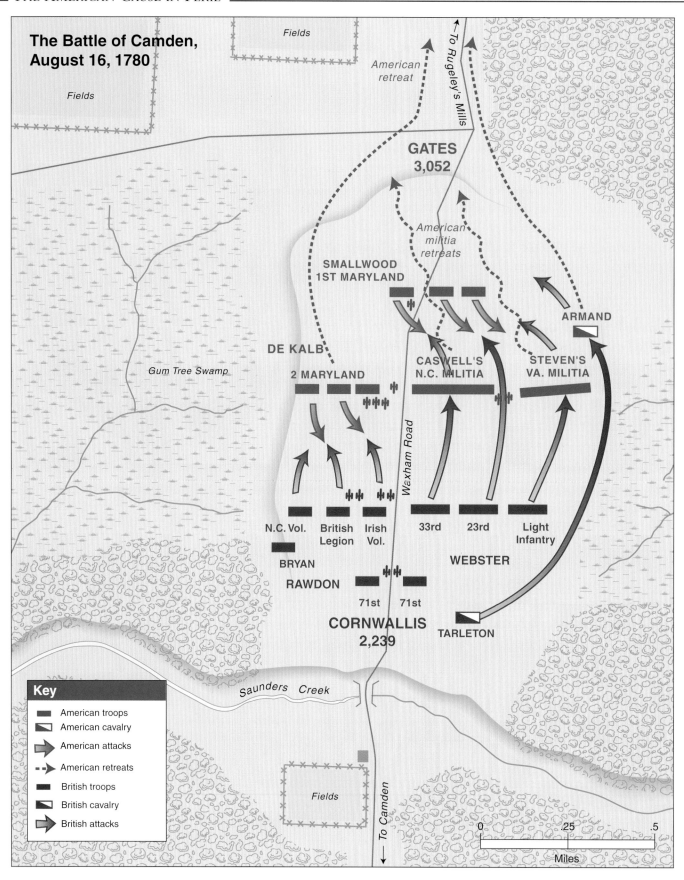

The Battle of Camden, August 16, 1780

Fields

Fields

To Rugeley's Mills

American retreat

GATES
3,052

American militia retreats

SMALLWOOD
1ST MARYLAND

ARMAND

DE KALB

Gum Tree Swamp

2 MARYLAND

CASWELL'S
N.C. MILITIA

STEVEN'S
VA. MILITIA

Waxham Road

N.C. Vol.   British   Irish
            Legion   Vol.

33rd   23rd   Light
                    Infantry

BRYAN

WEBSTER

RAWDON

71st   71st

CORNWALLIS
2,239

TARLETON

Saunders Creek

Key

American troops
American cavalry
American attacks
American retreats
British troops
British cavalry
British attacks

Fields

To Camden

0   25   .5

Miles

Once it became light, the British attacked. The Continentals, led by Kalb, fought splendidly and stopped the British advance against the American right. But the militia broke and ran at first contact. Many never fired a shot. A Virginia militiaman wrote: "I must confess I was amongst the first that fled. The cause of that I cannot tell, except that everyone I saw was about to do the same. It was instantaneous. There was no effort to rally, no encouragement to fight. Officers and men joined in the flight. I threw away my gun."

The rout of the militia allowed the British to turn and attack Kalb's soldiers in the flank. Inspired by Kalb, the Continentals continued to fight hard. Kalb received eleven wounds, one of which proved mortal. When he fell, the surviving Continental soldiers broke. Tarleton led the pursuit of the defeated patriots. Tarleton wrote, "After this last effort of [the] continentals, rout and slaughter ensued in every quarter." By 6 A.M. the battle was over.

The Battle of Camden was the worst defeat in the field (not in a fort or city) suffered by the Americans during the war. In less than one hour Gates's army had been wrecked. There were no accurate records of American losses, but only 700 men showed up when the survivors rallied at Hillsboro, North Carolina. Cornwallis lost 324 men. In the words of John Marshall, a Continental officer who later became a Supreme Court justice, "Never was a victory more complete, or a defeat more total."

Militia who had been marching to join Gates heard about the defeat. Many simply turned around and went home. Others switched sides and decided to support the British. They looted wagons carrying supplies for Gates's army and even attacked some of the rebels who were fleeing from the battle.

The defeat was especially embarrassing for Gates. During the first part of the battle he had been swept to the rear when the militia routed. Gates continued to the rear and did not stop until he reached Hillsboro. His retreat took three and one-half days and covered 200 miles. Gates claimed that his rapid flight was necessary because Hillsboro was the only place where he could rally new forces and continue the campaign. His enemies believed he had panicked and was a coward. Alexander Hamilton

wrote, "Was there ever an instance of a general running away as Gates had done from his whole army?"

Americans Fight Americans

More than anyplace else, the war in the south featured Americans fighting Americans. No one knew how many people considered themselves rebels and how many stayed loyal to King George. If the rebels controlled an area, the people who lived there said that they supported the patriot cause. If the British controlled an area, the people said that they were loyalists.

The rebels controlled the state governments. The state governments in the south put pressure on all able-bodied males to join the patriot militia. For example, in North

Above: British soldiers bayonet Johann Kalb (lying on the ground in middle) while British cavalry hack at fleeing rebel soldiers.

Opposite: A group of Tories holding a secret meeting in a cellar. Such secrecy was necessary. An American woman wrote during the Revolution, "...parties of armed men rudely entered the town, and [a thorough] search was made for tories."

Carolina adult men had to take an oath: "I will bear faithful and true allegiance to the State of North Carolina and will to the utmost of my power support and maintain, and defend the independent government [of North Carolina] against George the Third, King of Great Britain." If men did not take the oath, the government treated them as traitors.

People whom the patriots thought were loyal to King George were badly treated. In Georgia a patriot mob attacked Thomas Brown, tied him to a tree, and beat and kicked him until he passed out. An eyewitness remembered that the mob "burnt his feet, tarred, feathered and cut off his hair." Brown's feet were so badly burned that he lost two toes. The mistreatment of the loyalists made many of the loyalists want revenge.

One of the reasons the British invaded the southern states was that they expected to find support from loyalists. The former royal governors of Georgia and South Carolina told British officials "that if a proper number of troops were in possession of Charleston . . . or if they were to possess themselves of the back country [through] Georgia, and to leave a garrison in the town of Savannah, the whole inhabitants of both Provinces would soon come in and submit." British Major General James Robertson agreed. Robertson said that the southern Tories were waiting for the army to arrive to "enable the loyal subjects of America to get free from the tyranny of the rebels."

After the British gained control of Georgia and South Carolina, they faced the same problem that the Americans had faced: how to tell rebels apart from loyalists. Like the rebel state governments, Clinton tried to solve this problem by using the law. On June 3, 1790, he issued a proclamation that said that anyone who did not actively support the British was considered an enemy. Such a person was outside the protection of British law. To separate the loyalists from the rebels, people had to take an oath of allegiance to the king.

Clinton's proclamation was a serious step. Until now the organized forces on both the British and rebel side had tried to fight the war according to certain rules. Those rules included the protection of people who were not part of the fighting. Clinton's proclamation took away that protection. It angered southern patriots. Many decided that if the British were not going to fight according to the rules of war, then they would also ignore those rules.

Professional soldiers usually obeyed what were called the laws of war. Officers on both sides considered themselves gentlemen, and they tried to behave in an honorable way. By controlling their men, the professional officers controlled brutal behavior. But armed forces on both sides operated in the south without the control of professional soldiers. They were called partisans (guerrillas). They took up arms to make hit-and-run raids and then disappeared into hiding. Because they were outside anyone's control, many of them behaved with great brutality.

William R. Davie was a famous partisan leader who fought on the rebel side. On August 1, 1780, his men surprised a group of Tories at Hanging Rock, South Carolina. Davie trapped the loyalists between his rebel dragoons (soldiers on horseback) and his infantry. Davie described what took place: "The astonished Loyalists fled...and were charged by the dragoons in full gallop and driven back in great confusion; on meeting again the fire of the infantry they all rushed [wildly] against the angle of the fence where in a moment they were surrounded by the dragoons who had entered the field and literally cut them to pieces." In other words, Davie's men did not take any prisoners, but killed everyone instead.

Another famous partisan leader was 45-year-old Thomas Sumter. Sumter fought with such spirit that he received the nickname the "Carolina Gamecock." After the capture of Charleston Sumter suspected that the British would move inland. He left his home, sent his wife and son away for safety, and began raising volunteers. When Tarleton's men arrived at Sumter's home, they burned it down. They continued to hunt for Sumter and found instead the place where Sumter's wife and son had gone into hiding. They forced Mrs. Sumter to watch while they burned the house to the ground. This just made Sumter more determined to punish the British.

Sumter practiced what became known as "Sumter's Law." He had his men take whatever they needed from

William Davie was a bold and active partisan leader.

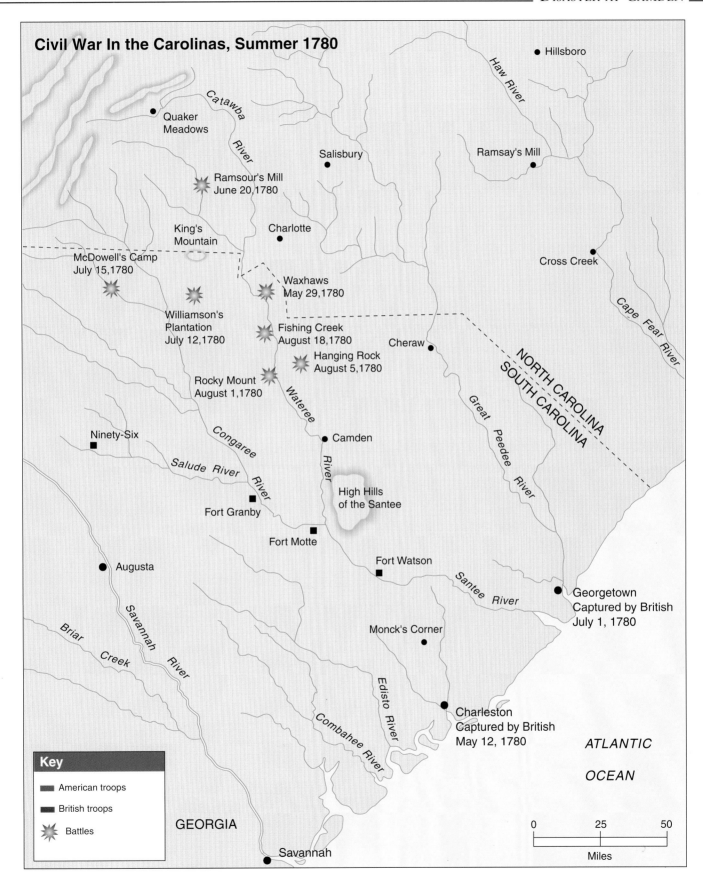

Civil War In the Carolinas, Summer 1780

Hillsboro

Quaker
Meadows

Catawba River

Haw River

Salisbury

Ramsay's Mill

Ramsour's Mill
June 20, 1780

King's
Mountain

Charlotte

Cross Creek

McDowell's Camp
July 15, 1780

Waxhaws
May 29, 1780

Cape Fear River

Williamson's
Plantation
July 12, 1780

Fishing Creek
August 18, 1780

Cheraw

NORTH CAROLINA
SOUTH CAROLINA

Hanging Rock
August 5, 1780

Rocky Mount
August 1, 1780

Wateree River

Great Peedee River

Ninety-Six

Camden

Congaree River

Salude River

High Hills
of the Santee

Fort Granby

Fort Motte

Augusta

Fort Watson

Santee River

Georgetown
Captured by British
July 1, 1780

Savannah River

Briar Creek

Monck's Corner

Edisto River

Charleston
Captured by British
May 12, 1780

ATLANTIC

OCEAN

Combahee River

Key

American troops

British troops

Battles

GEORGIA

0   25   50

Miles

Savannah

both captured prisoners and from people suspected of being loyalists. He rewarded his men by letting them share the things they took from the loyalists, including their black slaves. Sumter planned a series of hit-and-run raids against the British outposts in the Carolina back country. During July and August 1780 Sumter's partisans made many successful surprise attacks.

On August 6 Sumter led about 800 North and South Carolina partisans against a Tory camp at Hanging Rock. At first the rebels surprised the Tories and drove them back in confusion. But the British rallied around units of Tarleton's Legion. They formed a square (a boxlike formation with soldiers facing outward in all four directions) and bravely held their ground. Many of the rebels showed more interest in plundering (stealing from) the Tory camp than in fighting. After four hours Sumter ordered a retreat. His men had inflicted about 200 casualties and taken 70 prisoners while losing fewer than half that many.

After the Battle of Camden (August 16, 1780) the British got a chance for revenge against Sumter. Banastre Tarleton, who had not been at Hanging Rock, led a force of 100 dragoons with 60 infantry riding double to find Sumter. On August 18 he attacked Sumter at Fishing Creek. Although Sumter had about 800 men, they were sleeping, bathing in the creek, drinking, and lounging about their camp. The surprise was complete. Tarleton's men hit the camp before Sumter's men could collect their weapons. Tarleton inflicted 150 casualties and captured 310 men, 800 horses, 2 field guns, and 46 loaded wagons. He also freed 150 British prisoners. Sumter himself barely escaped by riding to safety bareback while leaving behind his hat, coat, and boots.

The partisan war in the South continued, a brutal war of burning, raid, ambush, terror, and revenge. A North Carolina militiaman described one act of revenge: "I was invited by some of my comrades to go and see some of the prisoners. We went to where six were standing together. Some discussion taking place, I heard some of our men cry out, 'Remember Buford' [the patriot leader of the forces whom Tarleton had destroyed at Monck's Corner] and the prisoners were immediately hewed to pieces with broadswords."

Nancy Morgan Hart performed many patriotic deeds, including dressing up as a "crazy man" to spy on the British in Augusta. According to legend, when six Tories entered her home to order a meal, she sent her 12-year-old daughter to warn her husband and then held the Tories at bay, shooting two of them. When her husband and neighbors arrived, they captured and hanged the rest of the Tories.

Opposite: Both sides behaved savagely during the partisan war in the south.

The rebel partisans forced the British to use many soldiers to guard the towns and forts they had captured in Georgia and South Carolina. The British also had to assign many men to protect their wagon trains that brought supplies to the field army. Every British soldier on guard duty was one less available to fight with the field army in a battle.

On the other hand, the partisans by themselves could neither defend the south's patriots against the British army nor drive the British away. They needed help from an organized force of professional soldiers. But during a period of only thirteen weeks Benjamin Lincoln had lost an army at Charleston, and Horatio Gates had been badly beaten at the Battle of Camden. By the end of August 1780 there were fewer than 1,000 Continentals at Hillsboro, North Carolina. They were too few and in too poor a shape to stop any attempted British invasion of North Carolina.

Mutiny in the North

The terrible winter at Morristown was very hard on Washington's army. Desertions and the discharge of soldiers who had enlisted in 1777 reduced the army's strength by about half. Yet the army, and in particular the medical service, showed some improvement during this difficult time. About 1,850 soldiers had died at Valley Forge during a mild winter. Only 86 died at Morristown in spite of the hard winter. The lack of food was the most difficult problem. Washington tried to explain to Congress that the army's situation was desperate: "Every idea you can form of our distresses will fall short of the reality."

On May 25, 1780, the situation threatened to get even worse. The army's supply system had broken down completely. The Connecticut soldiers had not received any meat for ten days. Two regiments came to evening parade in an angry mood. According to a Connecticut soldier, they were "growling like soreheaded dogs." When an officer tried to discipline them, a soldier shouted out, "Who will parade with me?" Most of the men in the two regiments at once began following this soldier instead of their officers. They intended to march off and leave the army. In military language such unlawful behavior was called mutiny.

The two regiments marched toward the camp of two more Connecticut regiments to encourage them to join the mutiny. If more soldiers joined the mutiny, the army was lost. If Washington's army fell apart, then the rebel cause would fail. Fortunately, some quick-thinking officers ran ahead of the disobedient soldiers and called the still quiet Connecticut soldiers to assemble without their weapons. Then the officers ordered loyal and armed soldiers to get between the soldiers and their huts so that they could not get their weapons.

A mutinous soldier stabbed a colonel with his bayonet. But officers were able to convince the soldiers to stop the violence and return to camp. Another colonel went to the men and convinced them to present their complaints in a disciplined way. Because the men respected that officer, they listened to him.

The mutiny of the Connecticut soldiers was an extremely dangerous moment. Washington reported to Congress that it "has given me infinitely more concern than any thing that has ever happened." Washington understood that hunger and Congress's failure to pay the men for more than five months had caused the trouble. He pardoned all except the most violent of the troublemakers.

Lafayette was away from the army when the mutiny took place. What he saw when he returned shocked him. Lafayette saw "An Army that is reduced to nothing, that wants provisions, that has not one of the necessary means to make war."

Congress shared the concerns of Washington, Lafayette, and his officers about the army's sad state. But Congress seemed powerless to make things better. Congress sent the individual states lists of what the states should provide the army. All too often the states ignored Congress. For example, in the spring of 1780 Congress ordered the states to send 16,500 recruits to fill the Continental regiments. Yet, by the middle of August only 6,000 recruits had come. It was the same with supplies. Congress requested the states to send supplies to the army. Some states sent supplies, others did not.

Washington, many of his officers, and some congressmen believed that Congress had given up too much power to the states. Now the states were preventing actions that were needed to win the war. The

Winter conditions at Morristown were much worse than the winter at Valley Forge.

states were each acting on their own. Washington described this as "one head gradually changing into thirteen." The states expected the French to do the hard work and to provide the supplies for the army. In Washington's view the states competed not to see "which shall do most for the common cause, but which shall do least." Congress, in turn, lacked the forceful leaders who could convince the states to make sacrifices for the national cause, or the common good.

The outlook for the American rebels at the end of the summer of 1780 was gloomy. Everywhere patriots looked, they saw huge problems: Congress powerless; the states acting on their own; Continental money becoming worthless; Washington's army weak; Gates's army in the south nearly destroyed at the Battle of Camden. George Washington's brother asked him how he could endure through such frustrating and difficult times. Washington answered, "There is one reward that nothing can deprive me of, and this is, the consciousness of having done my duty."

Revolutionary Medicine

The Continental Congress organized a Hospital Department for the army in July 1775. Like the rest of the army, the department lacked the supplies and people it needed to do its work. About 1,400 physicians cared for American soldiers, but only about 200 of them had graduated from a medical school. Medical care for soldiers was not considered very important in the army, in part because medicine of the time had little to offer. Diseases were treated with primitive practices such as bleeding (draining blood from a patient) or blistering (causing blisters by putting harsh chemicals on the skin). When a Continental soldier was wounded in battle, his wounds might be bandaged with pieces of an old tent. Surgery, most often amputation, was performed with dirty instruments and without anesthesia. A small number of useful medicines had been discovered, but the army did not have nearly enough in supply.

More soldiers died of contagious diseases that spread through dirty and overcrowded army camps than died from battle wounds. Sometimes at least half of the men in the army were sick or wounded and unable to fight. Many soldiers caught smallpox. Typhoid, spread by dirty drinking water, and typhus, spread by fleas and lice, also killed many soldiers. Doctors did not yet understand that invisible germs caused disease. That knowledge was almost 100 years in the future. Hospitals were even more dangerous places than camps for catching diseases. Already weakened by sickness and injury, men were crowded together in small rooms that were either too cold or too stuffy. Even when patients were put in houses, churches, or barns, many did not recover because of the poor care they received.

Chronology

THE WAR ON THE WESTERN FRONTIER

1775: The first permanent English settlement is established in Kentucky.

1776: Kentucky becomes a western county of Virginia. Its population will rise to 28,000 within a year.

July 4, 1778: George Rogers Clark and Virginia militia capture the British post at Kaskaskia, Illinois, without a fight.

July 20, 1778: The French settlement of Vincennes, Indiana, agrees to surrender to Clark's force.

December 17, 1778: The British retake Vincennes, again without a fight.

February 25, 1779: After a bold winter march Clark retakes Vincennes from the British.

THE WAR IN THE NORTH

July 3, 1778: In an event known as the "Wyoming Massacre" Tories and Indians attack and terrorize rebel troops and civilians in the Wyoming Valley of Pennsylvania.

July 18, 1778: Mohawk Indians led by Joseph Brant burn the white settlement of Andrustown, New York.

September 13, 1778: A force of Native Americans and Tories raids and burns the town of German Flats, New York.

October 8, 1778: Patriots destroy the Indian town of Unadilla, New York.

November 11, 1778: Indians and Tories massacre the settlers of Cherry Valley, New York.

May 31, 1779: The British capture the post at Stony Point on the Hudson River north of New York City.

June 15, 1779: In a surprise attack the Americans recapture Stony Point and later decide to abandon it.

August 11–12, 1779: Americans attack the British fort at Penobscot Bay, Maine, and lose a large number of men and ships.

August 19, 1779: In another surprise attack the Americans capture Paulus Hook, New Jersey, across the Hudson River from New York City, and then decide to abandon it.

August-September 1779: General John Sullivan leads Continental troops through western New York, burning Indian villages and destroying their crops.

December 1, 1779: Washington's Continental Army goes into winter quarters at Morristown, New Jersey.

May 25, 1780: After a hard winter Connecticut soldiers mutiny at Morristown.

THE WAR IN THE SOUTH AND AT SEA

January 29, 1779: The British capture Augusta, Georgia.

March 3, 1779: General Benjamin Lincoln and his troops are defeated by the British at Briar Creek, Georgia.

April 12, 1779: Spain forms an alliance with France, which helps the American cause by tying up a large part of the British navy.

June 16 and July 4, 1779: In the West Indies the French capture the islands of St. Vincent and Grenada from the British.

August 1779: The Spanish and French navies gain control of the English Channel and the waters off the coast of England.

September 1779: Admiral d'Estaing and the French fleet arrive off the coast of Georgia, capture several British ships, and, joined by American forces, begin a siege of Savannah.

October 9, 1779: French and American forces jointly attack Savannah, Georgia, and are defeated by the British.

February 11, 1780: After a difficult voyage from New York General Clinton's British troops land near Charleston, South Carolina.

April 8, 1780: The British surround Charleston.

May 12, 1780: The Americans surrender Charleston and 5,500 troops to the British.

August 16, 1780: The Americans are badly defeated at the Battle of Camden, South Carolina, by the British under the leadership of Cornwallis. The defeated General Gates flees to North Carolina.

Glossary

ALLIES: nations that are fighting on the same side in a war; used in this volume to mean the nations fighting against the British during the period of the American Revolution

BLAZE: to mark a trail through the wilderness by making cuts in the bark of trees along the way

CAMPAIGN SEASON: the period of milder weather, from spring through fall, when armies could march to battle; armies used to stop fighting and go into winter quarters during the coldest months.

COLUMN: an army on the march, arranged in ranks as wide as the road on which it is marching

CONFEDERATION: permanent alliance

CONTINENTALS: soldiers serving in the regular American army

DISARM: to take away weapons by force

DRAGOONS: soldiers who fought either on horseback or on foot

FEINT; FAKE: a movement of troops meant to fool the enemy about what an army is doing

FORTIFICATIONS: defensive structures, such as walls and forts, equipped with weapons

FRONTIER: the borderlands between European settlement and Native American lands in North America; the western edge of British settlement in the American colonies

GARRISON: the group of soldiers stationed at a fort or military post

GUERRILLAS: a small group of fighters who make sneak attacks in areas away from the armies and battlefields

MUTINY: an attempt by soldiers or sailors to overthrow their officers

PARTISANS; GUERRILLAS: fighters who were not part of the militia or army

QUARTER: mercy to a surrendered enemy; to give quarter is to spare the life of an enemy who has surrendered or to allow an enemy to surrender

RAID: a surprise attack on a military base or a civilian settlement; often involves stealing or destroying food, supplies, and property

RALLY: to encourage and reorganize soldiers who have become discouraged and disorganized

RENEGADE: traitor; one who abandons one's own people

TORIES: American colonists who sided with England during the American Revolution; also called loyalists

WEST INDIES: the islands of the Caribbean Sea, so called because they were once thought to be a part of India

WINTER QUARTERS: where armies camped during the winter

Further Resources

Books:

Boatner, Mark M., III. *Encyclopedia of the American Revolution*. Mechanicsburg, PA: Stackpole Books, 1994.

Furbee, Mary R. *Women of the American Revolution*. San Diego: Lucent Books, 1999.

Rankin, Hugh F., ed. *Narratives of the American Revolution as told by a young sailor, a homesick surgeon, a French volunteer, and a German general's wife*. Chicago: Lakeside Press, 1976.

Wilbur, C. Keith. *Revolutionary Medicine, 1700–1800*. Old Saybrook, CT: Globe Pequot Press, 1997.

Wilbur, C. Keith. *The Woodland Indians*. Old Saybrook, CT: Globe Pequot Press, 1995.

Yue, Charlotte and David Yue. *The Wigwam and the Longhouse*. Boston: Houghton Mifflin Co., 2000.

Zeinert, Karen. *Those Remarkable Women of the American Revolution*. Brookfield, CT: Millbrook Press, 1996.

Websites

http://library.thinkquest.org/10966/
The Revolutionary War—A Journey Towards Freedom

ushistory.org/march/index.html
Virtual Marching Tour of the American Revolution

http://www.pbs.org/ktca/liberty/game/index.html
The Road to Revolution—A Revolutionary Game

http://www.pbs.org/ktca/liberty/chronicle/index.html
Chronicle of the Revolution
Read virtual newspapers of the Revolutionary era

http://www.nps.gov/morr/
Official website of Morristown National Historical Park

Places to Visit:

Fort Moultrie National Monument, Sullivans Island, South Carolina

Morristown National Historical Park, Morristown, New Jersey

About the Authors

James R. Arnold has written more than 20 books on military history topics and contributed to many others. Roberta Wiener has coauthored several books with Mr. Arnold and edited numerous educational books, including a children's encyclopedia. They live and farm in Virginia.

Set Index

Bold numbers refer to volumes; *italics* refer to illustrations

Acknowledgments

Architect of the Capitol: 38–39

Eldridge S. Brooks, *The Century Book of the American Revolution*, 1897: 49

Anne S. K. Brown Military Collection, John Hay Library, Brown University, Providence, Rhode Island: Front cover, 50–51, 60–61

Charles C. *Coffin Boys of '76*, 1876: 54

Chicago Historical Society: 20–21

Lewis Collins, *History of Kentucky*, 1878: 11

Rudolf Cronau, *The Army of the American Revolution and its Organizer*, 1923: 27

William Hayden English, *Conquest of the Country Northwest of the River Ohio*, 1896: 12T

Harper's Weekly: 24B

Independence National Historical Park: 24T, 31, 36, 39, 55, 57, 62

Library of Congress: 8, 9, 14, 18, 19, 22–23, 25, 26T, 28, 29B, 32–33, 34, 37, 38, 40, 41, 53B, 56, 61B, 64–65, 66–67

Military Archive & Research Services, England: 6–7

National Archives: 13, 15T, 15B, 16B, 21, 26B, 30, 48, 53T

National Park Service: 44–45, 47 paintings by Don Troiani

New York Historical Society: Title page, 34–35

U.S. Government Printing Office: 16T

U.S. Marine Corps, Washington D.C.: 12–13 *Willing's Marine Expedition February 1778*, by Charles Waterhouse, 42 *Assault at Penobscot 28 July 1779*, by Charles Waterhouse

U.S. Naval Academy Museum, 50

U.S. Naval Historical Center, Washington, D.C.: 29T, 42–43

U.S. Senate Collection: 10–11, 16T

Maps by Jerry Malone